THE POWER OF
OF
MEDITATION

KAMESHA & ZACHARY SEAGLE

Balboa Press books may be ordered through booksellers or by contacting:

Balboa Press
A Division of Hay House
1663 Liberty Drive
Bloomington, IN 47403
www.balboapress.com
844-682-1282

Because of the dynamic nature of the Internet, any web addresses or links contained in this book may have changed since publication and may no longer be valid. The views expressed in this work are solely those of the author and do not necessarily reflect the views of the publisher, and the publisher hereby disclaims any responsibility for them.

Any people depicted in stock imagery provided by Getty Images are models, and such images are being used for illustrative purposes only.
Certain stock imagery © Getty Images.

ISBN: 979-8-7652-4711-2 (sc)
ISBN: 979-8-7652-4710-5 (e)

Library of Congress Control Number: 2023921564

Print information available on the last page.

Balboa Press rev. date: 11/30/2023

WE ARE MAGIC

THE POWER
OF
MEDITATION

ACKNOWLEDGE

To my family, my biggest inspiration.

Once upon a time there were 2 little girls Cici and Dri who loved to play, have fun, explore, and go on many adventures. They woke up on Sunday to find it was snowing outside, it was cold but very warm and cozy inside their home. They loved to waking up to check on the animals Darwin, Pluto and Snuggles. They liked to make sure they all had a good night's sleep. Every morning they fill their bellies with fresh veggies and seeds to keep them growing strong.

Ciara asked Dri "What should we do today?" Dri said "lets make a list". They had a long list of things: Eating, gaming, snacks, dolls, snow angels, snow ball fight, watch some TV,a movie.

They agreed toto allow each other to take turns picking something on the list... by the time each one picked 1 item, then soon ended up doing our own separate things. Cici went play with her horses and Dri when to watch some TV.

As time went by, they decided to stop and grab a snack. They both had big smiles on their faces as they enjoyed the sweet, juicy watermelon, and pineapple. In the living room they could hear daddy also enjoying the snack saying "man this is so good". When they finished their snack they went back to playing. Cici got bored with playing horses so she went to her room to play with dolls and Dri went to play with her room to play on her Ipad.

Moments later Dri finds herself in Cici rooms playing with dolls and they decided to have a pillow fight. Cici grabs her donut pillow, Dri has her squishmallow. Whack, Bam!! Pillows are flying and the girls are laughing and giggling and having so much fun. Net thing you here SMACK, BAMMMMMMMMMMMM!! Dri had grabbed a pillow and she went to turn around and didn't realize that one of her pillow's grabbed a barbie doll and hit Cici across her face. Cici face turned so red she started to cry and put her face down on the pillow. She was angry and sad. As soon as Dri realized her sister was upset she replied, "I'm so sorry". Cici said "Why did you hit me?" Dri replied "it was an accident I didn't see the doll on the pillow. Cici was so upset, crying she got up and ran to tell mommy.

Running down the hall crying, she could feel her heart beating so fast. Dri is right behind her and very sad, because her sister is so upset, she begins to cry... As soon as Cici runs into the Kitchen is goes to her mom hugs her crying. Her mom cannot understand a word she is saying, her mom can feel her heart beating so fast, she is breathing so hard and unable to make a full sentence. "What happened" mom asked? They both began speaking at the same time, both crying. Mom raised her hand and spoke very calm "Girls was this an accident? Dri stated "yes". Mommy always had the right words to say in the right moments.

They were both so upset trying to speak and tell our parents what happened that we weren't even listening to each other. They just wanted to be heard. Their hearts beating so fast and we could hear our breaths getting louder and faster, louder and faster... Mommy said girls.........girls... I want each of you to stop we froze... and she looked us in the eye and said "just take a deep breath in for 3 seconds..... 1, 1000, 2, 1000, and 3 1000.... and out for 3 seconds.... 1, 1000, 2, 1000, 3, 1000.......

They felt a little relief, but their parents asked them to join them in living room. They knew it was time to meditate. Their parents always taught them that when you feel upset, emotional, and unable to have clear thoughts to meditate. It works every time. And they were right. The girls felt calm, and peaceful. Next they grabbed their pillows and blankets got cozy on the floor, their hearts still beating fast. For the next 18 seconds our parents ask to sit in silence and to focus on their breath. Many times, before they meditate, they sit and focus on their breathing. Their Dad taught them this technique when he came home from his military training. He explained to the girls how this breathing helped him be calmer stressful times.

Mom began to guide the children into a meditation. They all sat quietly in the living room. Mom asked everyone to be breath in deeply and exhale deeply, letting any thoughts come and go, focus on their breathe. Their mom stated, "in with ease, out with ease". Breathing Tip: Imagine your breathing be like ..smelling a rose on the inhale, and blowing out a candle on the exhale. As you breath in you see your belly rise and when you breath out you feel your belly lower and breath out your mouth). Mom repeated "allow our breath to flow in with ease and out of us with ease.

In with ease... (breathing in) out with ease (breathing out), as we began repeating this, we felt calmer, in with ease (breathing in), and out with ease (breathing out) the girls became more relaxed. In with ease (breathing in), out with ease (breathing out) they noticed their heart beating was slowing down, and their breaths were slower, calmer, and deeper. The girls felt better, they felt their mind, breath and body connected as one. They felt the love in their hearts and released all the pain and focused on the connection with the breath. Remember to breath friends...

We Are Magic, The Power of Meditation

Feel free to practice the breathing and meditation as many times as you like. IF We can do it, you can do it. Remember the Magic that is inside of you is always present.

Namenste....

Now the girls hope to share this practice with my more friends and children around the world. They have found a connection and understanding of how to enjoy life and experience the importance of listening and connection with their inner self. The connection with breath and feeling the love in our hearts. Its truly magical.

Printed in the United States
by Baker & Taylor Publisher Services